BODY ON THE WALL

BODY ON THE WALL

Michelle Wing

SADDLE ROAD PRESS

Saddle Road Press
Hilo, Hawai'i
http://saddleroadpress.com

Cover photograph and design by Don Mitchell

Author photograph by Jamie Clifford

ISBN 9780991395200
Library of Congress Control Number: 2014930015

Some of the poems in this book have appeared previously in
this or other versions in the following publications or venues:
*The Gay & Lesbian Review, Sinister Wisdom, Redwood Writers
Anthology 2013: Beyond Boundaries, Redwood Writers Anthology
2012: Call of the Wild, Healdsburg Literary Guild Valentine's Day
Chapbook 2013: Let Me Count the Ways..., Healdsburg Literary
Guild Valentine's Day Chapbook 2012: Coffee, Chocolate & Verse,*
and *Creating Freedom: The Art & Poetry of Domestic Violence
Survivors* (California Museum, Sacramento, California).

Dedicated to Sabrina

for re-teaching me the meaning of home

Contents

EARTH

WATER

The Elements: A Four Part Incantation

I.   Sky reveal my pathway.
Extract the slender grey
of navigation from midnight stars.

Is it a northern passage?
Or will I awake
again tomorrow as a lost soul?

II.   Murmur soft sparrow.
Yours is not the fire of the phoenix.

Yet so much beauty
in a single feather,
in each note
of simple song.

III.   A wolf vanishes in night.
Follow him with pine boughs.
Cry low.
Find despair.

Day blooms morning after
like a sigh.

IV.   Remember water.
Not the pool, not
the cascade from the cliff —

this bead on your fingertip,
containing all the world,

and in a blink, gone.

I. WIND

風

"...who I was does not interest me. Who I am in the process
of becoming is strange and breathtaking to me.
To tell the truth I am scared to death. It is delicious."

—Helene Cixous, *The Book of Promethea*

How to Free a Poem

Winnow some words, toss them in the air,
waft the dead ones away
like so many boll weevils in the breeze.

Host a contest for the best first line
at the county fair, have Miss Cloverdale
read the winner to practice her elocution.

Camp out all night next to that spot in the backyard
where the dog loves to dig, meet those who live there,
swap marshmallows for their legends.

Hold your favorite writing pen up in the sky
at the moment the light disappears behind
the hills, and catch every bit of pink in the ink barrel.

Bundle up for a cold morning in the Mission District,
hold out a paper coffee cup on the street corner,
"Brother, can you spare a rhyme?"

Weave corner to ceiling in your writing den
with a ball of honey-soaked twine, then
sit like a spider, wait for flying images.

Open the door of the neighbor's barn, the hayloft,
and pitchfork the greenest adjectives,
the ones that make you dizzy with desire.

Visit your grandmother on bingo night,
fill the barrel with metaphors, play
poems with a blotter until you hit the jackpot.

Open a new page and leap in.

Body of a Woman, Cuerpo de Mujer

I learned love translated through the words of men
lifted and positioned by large rough hands
quiet and watchful from the smallness of my body
    I knew vulval curves, rose lips
    only through their eyes
        their possession
        their language.

Here, in a bare room on a single mattress
amber light from the street lamp
drifts through the decade of fog
    soft shadowing wine-wet lips
    illuminating my debut as
        the one who holds
        the one who touches.

Now I am the poet who marvels in wonder,
moaning with pleasure at her softness
encircling her wrist with my fingers
    breathing in her woman smell
    confusing my lips with her lips
        her lips with my lips
        sus labios, mis labios,
        nuestros cuerpos.

I found a language when I embraced her.

THE COMING-OUT WALTZ

She is a man in a felt hat
brown trousers, clean shirt
at a dance hall, dancing
with a mannequin in his arms.

She is a man in a felt hat
brown trousers, clean shirt
at a dance hall, dancing
with a doll that has no face.

She is a woman in a print dress
small flowers, lace collar
at a dance hall, dancing
with another woman,

an ordinary woman,
and the music whirls
around the room, around
their circle, as the heat

grows in their bodies,
until that moment
when she whispers,
The music's ending

but this dance
has just begun.

WORD PLAY

Poem bump bump bumping across the page,
    mirror is cool slick on cheekbones
        and your elbow smells of wet gardenias.

Walk in circles, walk in, circles,
    coil into my spine and stop
        sign a dance for us into the palm of my hand.

Move over, move under, take off your clothes,
    creep into the new night skin,
        soak in the hum drum drumming sound.

There is no high, no low, no midway or roadway,
    only the taste of lime on fingertips
        and a sharp true voice in a sky of birds.

STAR PEOPLE

I keep the star people
  in an old jam jar
tucked underneath my bed.

   Brush teeth.
   Drink water.
   Good night.
   No light.

Unscrew the lid, and here they come.
   Glitter
across each corner of my room,

land upon the bed post, on the dresser mirror —
   standing guard
   with their tiny swords.

WAITING

Your words come through the phone,
and I sweep them up with gentle hands
to drop them one by one into a glass jar,
preserving them
like peaches.

Anticipating succulence,
I wade slowly through spring days
into August heat,
heavy with longing. At last

I set the jar on the porch to warm
in three o'clock sunlight,
then serve you plump promises
in cool blue and white bowls.

SQUASH

Weeks ago
the garden withered.
Chill autumn mornings
flattened leafy plants.
Corn stalks, straw-colored, brittle,
bent earthward in the back row.

I stopped watering,
stopped looking,
stopped caring,
got ready —
to pull it all out
by the roots.

But yesterday,
sitting on the deck,
I spotted color
among the weeds,
ventured down
for one last look.

Beneath sprawling leaves,
summer
yellow —
elephantine
zucchini,
curved crookneck,
sunburst patty pan.

Like a jilted lover
changing old habits
too late to save
the affair,
my garden pleads
for one more dance.

What Is Seen

The vet took the little dog out of my arms,
placed her in the far corner of the room
and scattered chairs, waste baskets, tables,
before hitting the light switch.
Only a red bulb stayed on.
"Call her now," she said.

At two a.m.,
at our third emergency clinic
after nearly four hours in the car —
I watched her wince
in pain from the pressure
behind her eyes.

I said her name.
She moved towards me
and hit her head on a chair.
She turned, thumped into a waste basket.
"Call her again," the vet said.
I began to cry.
"Baby, here."

She tilted her head to one side,
backed up, found the wall.
Using its touch
against her shoulder,
she walked the perimeter.
Her nose pushed into my hand
— "Ah, here you are!"

When eyes fail us,
our hearts can still see.

ACCIDENTAL LOVE

As I lie against your chest,
look up into those
        cerulean sky eyes,
I do not understand it —
but my skin rests warm on yours,
my pulse runs strong,
and I do not want to lose
        the sweet scent of you
        on my sheets.

Passion enters the body
through unexpected doorways
and leaves me stunned.

ROMANCE FOR STRINGS IN THREE MOVEMENTS

I.   Nadja   *con bravura*

Alone in my living room,
CD jackets strewn
across the floor,
I fell for her first
as that violin's voice.
Now after years of longing,
this tiny figure stands
far from my balcony seat,
embodied at last.
The conductor beckons,
and strings sound.
Nadja fills the auditorium,
rising on a crescendo wave.
Allegro moderato, that sweet *andante*,
ending with *allegro vivacissimo*.
The final slice of the bow
pushes me up
into a manic "Bravo!"
my fist punching the air.
A woman front row and center
has slept through the entire movement –
she has obviously never
been in love.

II.   Daria   *con molta passione*

The cool stucco of a wine cave,
a musky taste of cabernet

tinges the night air.
Six heads nod. Six sets of fingers
poise on instruments' necks.
The downbeat comes, but
before the first measure is complete,
I am already lost,
mesmerized by
Daria's
legs.
Lime-green capri pants,
high-heeled shoes,
only a strap across the toes,
her skin bare from the arch of her foot
all the way up to that exquisite
curve of tensed calf.
Each bow stroke resonates
down through her body,
into those legs, as she pushes
against the floor
with her toes.
I chide myself to pay attention
to the notes
and not those
tantalizing shoes.
The man next to me seems
perfectly content to close his eyes,
let violins, cellos, violas,
exist in a world of sound, not sight.
I try but fail,
peeking from under my eyelids,
unable to separate the sextet
from the sex.

III.   Nina   *dolcemente, delicato*

It is clear, from the moment
she begins
this is all happening
just for me.
By chance, I land
in a front row seat,
Nina and her cello
twin goddesses before
my upraised eyes.
A diaphanous gown
cascades to the floor
like a night sky of shooting stars.
She embraces the curves with her knees,
leans into a downward stroke,
her long tresses cradling
that moon-glow face.
The notes sink into my lap,
caress my neck, whisper love.
My own chest aches at the sight
of her hollow-cheeked sadness,
and with each movement
I am further enthralled.
Pulled by the music,
I step up onto the stage,
take her in my arms –
the concert hall dissolves.

*Dedicated to Nadja Salerno-Sonenberg, Daria Adams, and
Nina Kotova*

Reclaiming the Rose

I will send you no valentine, no easy apology,
no tame cliché of pre-packaged romance,
and never those dozen long-stemmed corpses
morgue-cold and wrapped in plastic.

The rose I give is an explosion,
scarlet fever rises up from the stem,
evokes visions
and shivering.

This blood-spattered bush cries out
in the throes of transformation.
Here is wild passion, unbound
leaf by leaf.

READING CIXOUS IN TRANSLATION

Promethea sits in my lap
a book that is a woman
covered head to foot in a sheer veil
her beauty, her scent intoxicating
but her skin   the touch of her
        just beyond my reach.

As much as I stretch my fingers towards her
even when I am about
to cup   her breast   in my hand
it is not her breast
only a vision of breast defined
by silk, made of cloth
        a weaver's interpretation.

I hunger for her.
I want to lick each word
put my tongue on the nouns
take the nipple of her poetry between my teeth
and bite   taste the salt
close my eyes and make long slow
mouthings of each phrase
pressing them up against the roof of my mouth.

II. Fire

火

"A mountain soars, a torrent of sentences
Syllables of flame stitch the rubble"

— Meena Alexander, *Aftermath*

HEAT

While her restaurant burns, she irons clothes.
Hiss of heat makes clean creases of control.
From memory, another fire glows.
While her restaurant burns, she irons clothes.
She knows exactly how this story goes.
There is one way to soothe her scorched soul.
While her restaurant burns, she irons clothes.
Hiss of heat makes clean creases of control.

BREATHING

I saw a picture of my three-year-old self today.
I am so beautiful
it stops my breath.

This terror is not a word — no language
can tell you where I go
when fear cuts my stomach,

when I can no longer touch my face
because the hands are huge and rough.
They are me and him at the same time
so where can I go?

I cut my arm with a shiny new blade
watch the flowing ribbons, find
comfort in the scars that criss-cross
my skin, a visible map of pain.

I cut my pancake into tiny pieces,
push them around the white plate,
sop up the syrup, trace patterns,
but cannot bring the fork to my lips.

I cut time four weeks ago
with a bottle of thirty pale blue pills
and several carefully planned beers.
I thought the last swallow was my last.

But instead an i.v. line coils in
the crook of my arm and
charcoal fills my bowels —
the clock ticking again.

I will always be that child.
One breath at a time.

REFOCUS

She arrives at the shelter
face purpled with blows
no luggage but a crumpled bag.
Even her words are shattered.

It is her third time.

She rests here,
heals broken bird wings,
then bows to that altar promise
as to a gem, a shining pearl,
the only light.

If only she could step
into her own radiance,
dazzle herself with tomorrows —
even a lone sparrow can sing.

WALKING ON EGGSHELLS

It starts with words.

The ones
that tear me apart,
cut and pierce,
make me doubt
my own mind,
wonder if there
ever existed, anywhere,
refuge.

Then it is objects.

The soup can
splattering
above my head,
the stool fracturing
under his fist,
the doorknob
ripping off beneath
the heel
of his boot.

When he finally
shakes me, snarling,
and hurls me
across the room —

at least I can
stop dreading
what will happen next.

EVEN A WOMAN

Every day I ran.

The dog and I alone on a hiking trail,
middle of the day, only our panting breath
and footsteps to break the silence. Although
she was not there, I ran from the nightmares,

away from shadows, tried to calm
the startle reflex that tightened
each muscle of my hunted body, quivering
until exhaustion gave me stillness

enough to return to the little cabin
in the woods where no one knew
how to find me. I was in hiding,
one of the disappeared. New town,

unlisted phone number, quit the job
I used to have because I could not afford
to leave any trace. I had shrunk again
into that victim role, the one abandoned

so long ago. This caught me off guard,
unprepared. My running shoes tossed
to the back of the closet. Weren't these
days locked in my past? I didn't know

a woman could be the bad guy too.
After months of bullying, tantrums
and road rage, a crumbling beneath
her harsh words and jealousies,

I found enough courage to leave.
And then the stalking began, a
car outside my apartment at night,
assaults at the gym, letters sent

to my boss, harassing phone calls,
the restraining order claiming I was
the one on the brink of insanity.
I came to court, hoping for justice.

The judge dismissed all charges.

My girlfriend weighed 115 pounds,
stood five feet, four inches tall.
They were all thinking, "What is she afraid of?"

But even a woman can make you run.

BODY ON THE WALL

They send me a slip of paper
Anger Management — Certificate of Completion
And his name.
As if.

As if twelve weeks of one-hour sessions,
of talking about his feelings,
of tips on counting to ten,
could make him into a new man —

could undo the damage.

I know too well he can con anyone:
Police. Lawyers. Landlords.
Me.

And this piece of paper is the last slap
I am ever going to feel.

I walk to my closet, and get my dancing dress,
the little black one that twirls when I move,
that reminds me of freedom and the time before.

Do you want to know what he is like?
I'll need some tools.

Scissors to slash the hemline.
Blades to rip open sleeves.

A lighter to torch the fluttering strips.
Dirty boots to grind out the flames.

Then a razor, to nick my forearm
so I can smear blood across his name
and pin that piece of paper to my ruined dress.

I bandage my arm, find a hanger —

It is my body on the wall, bruised and battered,
and nobody, nobody, can say they don't see.

I Saw the Oak Leaves Tremble

her legs splay in the dirt
the seed
sprouts
grows
erupts
into her body
impales the belly
pushes her upright
branches out
into her breasts
shoulders, arms
she is immobilized
powerless, rooted
her heart covered
by ring upon ring of wood

in seconds
after the assault
she is
a hard bark tree
made of scars with no voice

TULIPS

Can I see a little girl in her shimmery yellow party
dress break away onto the dance floor at a wedding,
spin among the male relatives and not panic? Can I
watch her twist and twirl — beautiful, light — and
trust her fairy soul is protected and safe? No.

I suspect nearly every man in the room. Could it be
him? Or him? Will he be the one? I follow her with
telescope eyes, and if I must, I get out of my chair to
keep her in my vision. Only when she is back in the
arms of an aunt, or nestled in a grandmother's lap,
do I relax.

Being a little girl is risky. It is dangerous. I failed
to avoid the perils. So as a large adult, a big person
with powers, I am on the lookout, ready for action.
Not on my watch is my mantra, if one must choose a
mantra.

My request? No emotional scars on victims, and real
scars on abusers. Instead of Hester Prynne's *A*, an *A*
for *Abuser* — right on the forehead in red letters. An
R for *Rapist* in purple on the left cheek.

No more hiding in the open. Instead of victims who
cower in fear, let perpetrators be afraid to show their
faces. Let them sit in their homes, social outcasts,
prisoners of their crimes. Let victims be free to walk
the streets.

When I am the queen,
the tulips will be purple.
Scars will brand rapists.
It is time for our freedom.
We will be fearful no more.

SHAME

Molten lava pours
from pen to page
a heat of remembrances
liquid fire.

I lick the shame
from my hands
plunge them
into the flames.

Burn. Burn it all.

DREAMWORK

In my dreams
I am learning to scream.

It has been years since I tiptoed
through my own house, years
since I trembled
when the phone rang,
since any slight
movement of a hand
made me flinch.

Here, no raised voices, no shattered plates.
No cowering on the floor of my closet,
wondering how I would make it
through one more episode
of the tawdry soap opera
my life had become.

When he threw me across the room,
I had forgotten how to cry out loud.
When the police stood before me,
I had no words.
When my family asked for explanations,
I had no answers.

It is here, now, in a house filled with love,
that the nightmares come.
Men torture dogs, strangle babies, rape women.
Violence churns black and thick,
traps me, renders me once again
silent, helpless.

But one night I push up out of bed
screaming, "No!"
A big, bold, strong voice.
A *Stop now don't look back I mean it!* voice.
Night after night, the dreams come,
and I scream.

No.   No.   No.   No.

Until finally. No more.

GIFTS

You come to me as electronic messages,
envelopes filled with lamentation
coursing through the air in search
        of a place to touch ground.

Stories of grief, of loss, of families
ripped apart, torn limb from limb, mothers bruised,
children terrified, fathers imprisoned by alcohol,
        legacies of pain.

And yet each missive arrives bundled
in courage, wrapped up with hope,
looking towards a future without
        hiding or fear.

One by one, I receive these offerings,
open my hands to hold them,
pull them in close to my chest,
        and breathe in thanks.

You are brave — I honor you.
You are resilient — I am humbled by you.
You are powerful — I draw strength from you.
        Each one of you is a gift.

*dedicated to all the Changing Hurt to Hope: Writers Speak Out
Against Domestic Violence contributors*

How I Became a Poet

after hurt
before healing
     rage —

I. art therapy

lie down on butcher paper
big fat marker tracing
outlines of my body

now
write down
the emotions.

head crazy
with thought words:
anxiety, despair, suicide.

stomach, chest
hold lost/scared/alone.

afterthought:
deep in the gut
tiny spiral
controlled print — rage.

II. night at the movies

what are friends for?
no more good girl,
she says, giving me video
of lesbo soft porn shorts.

alone, pop it into the VCR
third movie — S&M scene,
ugly names, rough sex, pseudo

rape. freeze.

eject. get a hammer,
smash the case and pull,
pull, pull
miles of tape,
until i sit in a sea of smut.

III. behind the curtain

hear voices outside
the two-story apartment
a man, foul, harsh.

race to the window
and see him throw

her hard onto the asphalt.
i am on the concrete balcony,
scream, stop!
stairs are too far.

balanced, ready to jump
— but
my buddy grabs me from behind
whispers no, this ain't the way, baby.

this ain't the way.

too late...the man pushes her
into a car, drives, gone.

IV. fire escape

san francisco three p.m.
sixteenth and mission
sunny day, people everywhere.

fire escape drops down
as i walk by a little shop
no one notices.

i step into shadows, watch —
man hits ground first, holds woman's
wrist: short skirt, bruised arms/legs

yanked to sidewalk, then
out into traffic
begging let go, let go.
no   one   sees
no   one   hears

i follow, cut
through traffic, to head
of alley, biggest voice i have
hey buddy!

he stops. i say *let her go.*
he says *you don't understand –*
i stand firm, like a fuckin'
cowboy in some Western.

hesitation, but he lets her go.
i turn back to the street
see twenty people, impromptu
posse, how goddamn cool is that.

V. take-out

she holds shitty little
cardboard box
of food, *here?*

wham! he knocks
it out of her hands
to the pavement –

so what next? of course,
that i'm so sorry look
on her face, the one i
know so well, can

hear her apologizing
while he big bully
storms at her.

i drive alongside
need a ride? at first,
no, but when i stay nearby,
when brute/man gets nasty

again, i swing open
the door and this time

she gets in.
his face
is a too-full balloon,
red hot ready to explode
but right now, car door
shuts, and we two,
women-allies, are safe.

VI. warpath

i walk city streets
dressed in black
motorcycle boots
black jeans, black jacket
bristle with rage
ninja warrior girl.

118 pounds
ready to fight
anybody   anywhere

it eats me up
i go inside hollow
nothing there
just lemon-bitter/lonely.

VII. different tool box

maybe i helped
sometimes but am
i really a superhero?

answer: nope. mere mortal.

next question —
is it possible for me
to become someone
instead of simply
to survive?

it is time
for a new game plan:

i must fill up
my reservoir
search for hope
find compassion.

learn how to battle
with poems
instead
of hammers —

i will pick up
a pen, notepad

and write.

III. EARTH

土

"We all carry within us the place of our exile, our crimes and our ravages. But our task is not to unleash them on the world; it is to fight them in ourselves and others."

—Albert Camus, *The Rebel*

PERFECT

we had the nicest manners
the *yes please, no thank you,*
may i be excused
that impressed our parents' friends

and when the phone rang
my *hello, wing residence,*
this is michelle,
may i ask who's calling?
was the envy of all my father's clients

we were well behaved
in restaurants, choosing from the two
or three options given, eating
everything on our plates

at school, we did well,
steered clear of trouble,
respected our teachers,
turned in all our work

and every sunday,
there we were, filling
an entire pew,
six children in crisp new clothes,
bodies clean, hair glowing
from the previous night's bath.

we were perfect —
except

we weren't.

First Born

another day
as witness
to my mother's rage

the yelling,
the this-is-too-much!
be quiet!
stay out of my kitchen!
throwing food
onto plates

until I say,
*why did you have
so many children?*

angry words, but honest.

just as quick the reply —

*which ones do you want
to get rid of?*

some words you can
never take back.

IN THE CHICKEN COOP

three thousand chickens
and grandpa tired
from his day job

so my mom and her sisters
help gather the eggs.
Aunt Louise is nine

my mom seven,
the littlest one five.
they listen to *Fibber McGee*

and Molly, *Jack Benny*,
singing together
(during the good times,

since his nickname at work
was Happy, after all)
but the moods always came,

an argument, something
small, and then the eggs
became missiles, bombs,

smacked my aunt in the face,
she remembers —
a dozen or more

while she cried, begged him
to stop, the younger girls
frozen, my mom

in the middle praying
(i know this) the storm
would pass her by.

THE FENCE

My fourteenth summer,
my father gave us a project —
build a fence around twenty acres of land.
My California cousin and I

woke early that first July morning,
carried a sack of nails and two hammers
out into the field. We were slow, hefting
the rails one at a time against each post,

beginning to tap in the long spikes,
hesitant, arms unused to the motion,
foreheads wet in the growing heat.
But as the day stretched on, we learned:

how to brace our hips against the wood,
feel the rhythm, pound the nails in
with fewer strokes, use each other's bodies
to make the work quick, effortless.

Two weeks we labored, learning as much
about each other as we did about the knotted
pine.When our muscles shivered,
we leaned back against our fence, sipped cokes,

stared up at the Montana sky
that covered everything.
Then it was again to the task, rail by rail,
one hammer blow at a time.

We did it for the money, a nickel a nail.
But there is no memory of the paycheck
no recollection of whether it was spent
on record albums or roller skates.

What is left is the fence:
twenty acres of *I am*
stretching across the canyon's grasslands,
standing tall among the timothy.

REAL

That night standing under stars
when I traced my first constellation,
I wish someone had said, "That's Diana,
goddess of the hunt. See her bow, stretched taut?

The quiver of arrows? And those three stars,
look close — the pattern of her belt. Nearby,
her faithful dogs." But no, it was Orion.
Another god to fill the sky.

The children's books long since abandoned —
the *Velveteen Rabbit*, *Pinocchio*, searching
for a place in the world. Their message
had been clear: freedom lies in becoming

a real boy. Is it any wonder I kept a bag
packed with jeans and sweatshirts,
planned to bind my small breasts,
had chosen a new name?

with thanks to Tania

BELIEF

It's all the books, my mother said,
glancing towards my father for confirmation.
The Sunday school teacher nodded,
solemn, as discussion continued

over the sorry plight
of my soul. Seeking Presbyterian
answers to their dilemma —
their oldest child, refusing to do

this basic thing.
Because it was time,
now, for me to sip
grape juice with the adults.

In private, my teacher asked,
Are you smoking? Using drugs?
In trouble at school? Pregnant?
As if only impurity

could keep me from the Lord.
No one ever asked me
what triggered my hesitation;
and not once in those days

did anyone inquire
what book lay zipped up
in my backpack — a biography
of Robert Goddard,

father of modern rocketry,
who said,
The more I know about the universe
the more I believe in God.

WEDDING ALBUM

Here is the white dress,
the bouquet, sunlight
streaming through church

windows. Here are the flower
girls, guests holding plates
with wedding cake tiered

precariously, wine glasses
and silver ribbons, the packages
threatening to capsize

a groaning table, and everywhere,
everywhere, people
are dancing and smiling.

You cannot tell, turning
through these pages,
that she said, please,

a small, simple affair.
Not in a church. Maybe
a light snack, only a few

of our closest friends.
And no engagement ring —
just two plain gold bands.

64

She did insist on keeping
her name, said both parents
should walk down the aisle,

and a veil, really? What modern
woman hides her face?
And what does marriage

mean anyway? Do we
really want to do this?
No, this bride under lace

cannot be the woman
who ninety days before
stared at a bottle of pills

late into the night,
spent an early and solitary
honeymoon in a locked

ward. Because look at
her! How happy she is,
everything has gone

exactly as planned.
It's only here in one
picture you see a slight

hint of rebellion,
something out of place —
not looking at the camera,

as she waltzes with
a cousin, the veil gone.
There's a sun-reddened

outline visible on her back.
Damn the dress, she had said.
I'm teaching my sister to dive.

THAT ONE TIME

Rule number one: behave.

Rule number two:
(directly related to the above)
don't ever embarrass your mother.

Futile to say a teacher
treated me unfairly,
or a coach pushed too hard —
that a doctor wasn't listening,
or a Sunday school teacher
seemed misguided.

Except that one day, when she came
alone to my hospital room.

I was no longer a child.
After years lost and broken,
trying to get better, in and out
of psych wards and clinics,
I asked for help, checked
into a private institution
near their home.

She and my father visited, brought
lattes, tried to understand,
to make up for time, to learn
this new language.

But a few weeks into therapy,
my doctor declared I was an ideal
candidate for electric shock therapy —
not to worry, it's so much better
these days.

Mom found a different place,
other options, set things in motion.

As I waited for her that day, the doctor
swept into my room, large and angry.
Leaving was "against medical advice," he said,
then turned away as if I were an insect.

My mother found me in a small heap of tears.
Like a growling she-bear, out to the hallway
she went, in search of that man.

We checked out together,
her face still flushed with indignation.
Oh, my heart. What wild love was there.

PILLS

Capsules, caplets, round, oblong, pink, brown,
white, yellow, green, speckled, buff – twenty-eight
pills a day cupped in my hands. Pill boxes, pill
cutters, a deep drawer full of pill bottles in the
kitchen. Pill boxes in the glove box of our cars, in
my messenger bag, in the dog's tote, in the computer
case, any possible container going out of the house.
The eternal question — "Do you have your pills?"
And a bottle of water. That must be remembered,
too.

Some take pills only when sick, when they have
a cold or a headache, instead of being sick by
definition — by definition of the very pills carried
in this bag. As a child, I once spent the night at
the home of a friend whose mother sat frail and
quiet, wrapped in an afghan. In the morning, with
coffee, she opened her pill box with shaky hands,
different compartments for each day of the week, a
pharmacy's worth of medicines. I never asked what
was wrong.

Now, on Sunday evenings, restocking an identical
pill box, I think of her, especially on the days my
hands tremble.

> A mouthful of pills
> Noon, six and just at midnight
> Like a clock it goes
> Keeping my illness at bay
> Keeping my illness in mind.

69

Now I Lay Me Down

From a sound sleep, Hamlet's words
coursed through me in the darkness, and
I cried "to take arms against a sea
of troubles," my fist thrust in the air.

Last week, I careened through
a chain-link fence in my car,
and then pulled shards of glass
out of my dog's belly by hand.

Tuesday, when I was laughing out loud,
my wife wanted in on the joke —
the cats were revving their engines,
in preparation for the Daytona 500.

And at least once a month,
there is a baby lost, forgotten,
hurt, dead. Always the babies.
I am never in time to save them.

Each night, I strap in for the ride,
not knowing if it will be
the Mad Hatter's teacups
or Space Mountain.

A Trip to Vietnam

My sister sang
in her lilting voice
a schoolgirl's praise of a president:
Ho Chi Minh, Ho Chi Minh.

Five years before she came
to us, she wandered the streets
of Saigon, hungry and looking
for her mother.

The agency took a photo,
found some clothes,
gave her a birthday,
since four year olds aren't
good with details.

Before our first meeting,
I purchased children's stories
in Vietnamese, a gift
she accepted mutely,
but sat in the car for two hours
to devour the words.

She remained stoic in the midst
of our untranslatable noise,
drew pictures of the winged
creatures that kept her eyes
open even while she slept.

When we found her bed empty,
my mother learned to check the hutch
or large wardrobes, then coax
her back to the quilted vacancy
alongside her new sister.

After months of silence,
her first communication
was that the orphanage
had been stingy
with meat,
but always had rice
and vegetables.

A newlywed now,
she travels to a land whose
language no longer dances
on her tongue.

My sister holds
her U.S. passport
in honey-brown hands
and, like that child again,
searches for home.

What I'm Not Supposed to Write

I try to write poetry
but there are days when nothing
is very poetic.

The old blind dog, confused
by seizure drugs, bumps about
looking for an exit.

Our cat, once a tiny rescue
and last week diagnosed obese,
throws up on the piano.

Instead of sitting at my keyboard,
I pull off ticks, empty cat boxes,
and three times clean up
puddles of pee from the laminate.

Broken beaks, rattlesnake bites,
abscesses and swallowed objects,
midnight trips to the clinic —
I thought I was prepared for anything.

But when my father died, I still believed
in those obituary lines we read so often:
He passed away peacefully.
For I had cradled an animal in my arms
as it was put down.

Now, as I held his hand,
heard those last rales dehumanize him,
watched his body lurch under the sheets —
all I wanted was for the torture to stop.

At last it did.
Then a black magma spewed
out of his mouth.

Bless that nurse, whose name I don't recall —
the one who used a suction tube
to clear his lungs,
a cloth to wipe his face,
and disappeared,
allowing us to pretend, for the moment,
that it hadn't happened at all.

IV. Water

水

"I knew every raindrop by its name."

— Denis Johnson, *Car Crash While Hitchhiking*

Silent Winter Retreat: A Meditation in Haiku

Trees mist in morning.
Rabbit scampers up hill.
All this just for you.

Wood wind chimes in rain.
No knowing, no attachment
Inside the *zendo*.

One person swallows.
It ricochets down the room.
Twenty monks, one mind.

Okra and mushrooms,
Molasses sugar cookies —
Don't grasp or repel.

Imperfection's face:
I ache and squirm.
Around me, seated mountains.

Here in this moment
A taste of enlightenment —
Ah! Peppermint tea.

Who can contain time?
After hours spent in stillness
I finally let go.

Now in the darkness
All voices summon Buddha.
Chants play on night's face.

Ancestors, awake!
Show me how to live this life —
I humbly ask you.

Back to the basics:
breath, presence, compassion —
Yes, this is enough.

HIROSHIMA'S PSALM

America won.
Japan lost.
A city vanished.

Visitors today are awed
by its wide boulevards,
expansive parks,
this metropolis unlike any other
in the land of the rising sun
because there was a blank field
to build upon.

Welcome to the center of zero.

They call it Peace Park,
this place of the skeleton dome,
somber museum filled with black
and white photos of nothing.

School children with knapsacks
and crisp uniforms
come here to learn the most important
lesson of war:
Don't be in one.

What of those other children?
Where are their families?
What about Kenji and Midori?
The Nakamuras, the Kawabatas?

Here in the piles of rubble,
Shigeru's lunchbox,
Nobuko's summer blouse,
fistfuls of Hiroko's hair.

They are chrysanthemums.
They are memory.
They are row upon row
of creased paper cranes
taking wing after the last bomb falls.

ACROSS THE DIVIDE

We are strangers
waiting for our names to be called
at the free clinic.

We both fill out forms,
balance clipboards
on our knees.

We both look at our watches,
wonder if we will
miss an hour's pay.

We both wear clean clothes.
Mine are vintage thrift store.
Yours are cheap but new.

I feel your eyes scan my profile,
take in the difference,
not the likeness.

Somehow, my privilege
is etched deep
into my forehead.

My college education
rises along the ridge
of my nose.

My upper middle class
upbringing bleeds through
the calluses in my palms.

My parents' swimming pool
reflects out of the blue
in my eyes.

If you could see my intake form,
you would know I am walking
that same tense line.

But you don't trust me,
no matter what the paperwork
might say.

When my name is called first,
you look me full in the face,
then turn away.

KARMIC JUSTICE

The Buddhist precept says
refrain
from killing
and harming
living beings
but

as yellow jackets
descend
on my coffee cup
skim
the dogs' water bowl
swarm my ears

I succumb to
Old Testament roots
and wage war.

I bait
the yellow cone
of a wasp trap
with rank tuna
and wait.

One by one
they follow the oil smell
squeeze their bodies
up into the tip
and out
through the hatch
that has no exit.

Soon
the amber cage
crawls with thirty or
more frantic wasps

bumping each other
scaling the walls
circling in senseless
patterns of despair.

I go about my day
do chores
avert my eyes
avoid the site
of my crime.

When sun slips low
over twilit hills
the death dance
is nearly over
piles of bodies
stacked deep
in this
charnel house.

One wasp refuses
to fall on the corpses
of his brothers
wearily clings
to plastic walls
until he too must finally
stop the struggle.

I imagine I shall
come back
in my next life
as a yellow
and
black insect
knowledge of human
machinations
locked in an inaccessible
corner of my tiny
brain

that I will
smell tuna
one summer afternoon
and think only
"How delicious!"

ODE TO A LAUNDRY BASKET

I had gone through my share
of failed relationships,
colorful enticements bursting
into my life with fancy promises,
bright plastics and clever designs,
only to lie in cracked ruins
within months.

I was ready for commitment,
a partner, someone who
planned to be in it for the long haul.
So this time, I went searching
with a list of necessary qualities:
strength, reliability, natural beauty.
I wanted it all.

And there you were,
a classic, a Penelope, graceful
in your woven seagrass over a steel frame.
With allure enough to attract
a thousand lovers,
yet the steadfastness to wait
for the one who is coming home.

ZAZEN

Sometimes sitting zazen is like slipping in between clean sheets after a hot bath; other times, it's like rolling down a hill inside a metal trash can. — Debi Papazian, sangha sister

Pull out the *zabuton*, lay it down it in front of the altar, choose a stick of sandalwood incense to insert in the hand-glazed bowl. Set my timer for thirty minutes, light candles, ring the singing bowl from Tibet, bow three times.

Settle into the cushion. Rock slightly back and forth, find my center, place thumb against thumb, hands nestled against belly. Bring the gaze of my eyes down and begin, with the breath, the in, the out. Loosen the stiffness in my shoulders with a slight shrug; reposition. Breathe.

My foot cramps. A wiggle of the toes. Breathe. Still cramping. Flex, release, flex, release. The cramp moves up into my calf. Focus on the breath. My leg cries out for release, and really, is this a contest? I stretch out, rub the muscle, reposition, restart. Breathe. In, out. In, out.

Wait. Is it trash night? No, that's tomorrow. Damn. Thinking. Go back to the breath. In, out. In, out. Breathe.

My nose tickles. A good Buddhist should be able to ignore this. I am an iron bull, unmoving, tormented by a mosquito. I am not an iron bull. I scratch my nose. Reposition, back to my sitting posture, unmovable mountain.

Now the dogs are out in the backyard barking. They'll stop in a minute, right? I can't get up from my meditation to call them in. Ignore the dogs. Think of quiet. Quiet and barking dogs. Barking and barking and barking. The neighbors will not appreciate *zazen* as an excuse.

I give up and make a quick dash to the yard, call everyone in, lock the dog door. Back on the cushion, resettle. The grey cat walks into the room, jumps up onto the altar. I attempt to ignore her. She will go away. I am meditating. No more distractions. With a flick of her tail, she knocks over the vase holding the bamboo shoot. Water spills across the wood, pools around the base of the candles. I am up again, righting the vase, gathering paper towels, shooing the cat. But I am calm. I am Zen.

Here I am again, back on the *zabuton*, committed to my practice. Feeling the breath. In, out. In, out. Busy brain. Now I am thinking about a poem. I want to write down some lines, something about a pomegranate splitting open in the fall, because otherwise I might lose them. But I am in *zazen*. This is not allowed. Poets and Buddhists are at odds over this. It has yet to be resolved. I manage to reach paper and jot notes, without actually leaving the *zabuton,* as a compromise.

Okay. Now, where were we? Right. Breathing. Count breaths, get back into focus. On the out breath, up to five. That always works. How long have I been here,

anyway? I sneak a look at the clock. Twelve minutes?
I shake the clock to see if it is still working, which is
pointless, as it is digital. I start counting breaths again.
Too distracted. Can't even get past one.

Another strategy. Listen to sounds, focus on my sens-
es. I sink into my body. There is the gurgle of the fish
tank, the hum of the refrigerator. I hear the chitter of
a squirrel, the rap-a-tap of a woodpecker in a nearby
tree. There is a crunching noise. Just a dog toy,
probably. Not to worry. Breathe. More crunching. A
disturbing crinkly texture, something not right. A
cause for alarm. I must get up to investigate.

The Great Dane has stolen a bottle of liquid hand
soap, still in its packaging. I find her with bubbles on
her chin. Pick up the pieces, wash the dog's face,
head back to the cushion. This is the longest half hour
of my life. It will never end. I sigh, and once again
soften my gaze.

The incense is still burning, a steady scent of sandal-
wood. With a shift in light, the Buddha on my altar is
now glowing amber. Smoke spirals into the air.
Breathe. In, out. In, out. Counting. My service dog
relaxes at my side, her lungs expanding and contract-
ing in rhythm with mine. Everything goes soft and
sharp at the same instant. Candle flame sings psalms
only I can hear. Breathing. On the cushion.
I am present, full, now. This is it! Bliss! Like a crash-
ing waterfall, thoughts, emotions, judgments rush in
—and the moment is gone.

ANTHROPOMORPHISM

A woman in my writing group
warned me not to give
human emotions
to animals.

She spoke of the dangers
of anthropomorphism
as if it were a disease
my poem might catch
if the metaphors were not
properly sterilized.

Last week I saw
a fawn struck dead
by the side of the road.
I carried the image home
with me, mourned the loss.

But within an hour,
caught up in email messages,
grocery lists, phone calls, poems —
I had forgotten the baby deer.

The next morning
I saw the body again.
His mother was standing vigil.
She nuzzled him as I drove past.
Had she been there all night?
Did she pray for a return of life?

Or did she only hope
to keep scavengers away
for a few more hours?

Tell me, whose grief was more real?

Things That Stop My Breath

Raised bows before the first down stroke. A single harmonic note. The smell of Japanese incense. A kitten's sandpaper tongue. "I think I love you." The glacial water of a mountain lake. Chopin — anything by Chopin. Her lips at the back of my neck. Orange moonlight on an August vineyard. Crimson paint tearing across a large canvas. Stage fright at my first piano recital. The alarm clock, every morning. Hot coffee spilled in my lap. Shattered dish shards in the kitchen sink. A snake coiled at the base of the toilet. A lizard's tail under the sheets. "This file is corrupted." A power outage in winter. My ex's name on caller i.d. The splintered smash of a chair against the wall. Thud of a dog's body against my front bumper. "Your father has lymphoma." A razor opening the skin of my own wrist. The moment Anna throws herself under the train.

NATSUKASHII

My Japan
is the neighborhood greengrocer —
eggplant, *kabocha*, *daikon*,
sweet watermelon.
Hiyayako, silky taste at the tofu stand.
It is students in the subway,
gleaming like stars in fresh uniforms.
Taxi drivers in white cotton gloves,
making way for housewives on bicycles,
laden with shopping bags.
It is the snow of New Year's at shrines,
against a kaleidoscope of kimonos.
And, most of all, in the spring,
it is the nightly news, a weather report
with the pink line of cherry blossoms
gradually rising, *hanami*.

Natsukashii — nostalgia, homesickness.
Kabocha — Japanese pumpkin
Daikon — Japanese radish
Hiyayako — fine soft tofu, eaten cool in summer
Hanami — flower viewing, specifically of cherry blossoms.

LANDSCAPES

The hydrangea died and I cannot right
    this canoe carrying metaphors
        paddle against a current of stale
            images moving in trite waters
    music is absent
        forget the babbling brook   words
in a mountain stream   Walden   walled in
and out the café window I see
    tattooed bike messengers.

Smell of fresh mown hay succumbs to heat-heavy
    piss on concrete, your cow needs milking
        graffiti-bold news racks buckle
under the weight of skyscraper shadows
        next to buttercups
and the litter of hypodermic needles
    reused instead of traded.

I tried to write about tadpoles and meta-
   morphosis but the bus broke down
     human sweat stings my nostrils
       there is no room for a cardboard shanty
       town in the barn
       pay toilets flush automatically on school days
where farm boys learn arithmetic and proper
     use of condoms found in gutters with cigarette
        butts and timothy grass you can suck
for the sweetness.

The grocery cart stands on forty acres of loamy soil
and I lean heavy into the plow,
ripping up dark earth so the neon
will have a night to shine into.

IF YOU ASKED ME

I would tell you about the time
we sat outside with early-morning coffee,
and my ring slipped off my finger
down through a crack in the deck.

Because I was in my new pink leopard PJs,
she ventured into the three-foot crawl space
while I shone a flashlight from above.
And during that twenty foot trek,
as she traversed mud, scraped on rocks,
pushed aside clumps of clotted animal hair,
we laughed.

With color commentary, she entertained me,
included me in the spelunking adventure,
as she found the two cat bowls, missing
since the raccoons ran off with them,
and an almost empty bag
of dog food, plus a mysterious bone.

When at last she emerged from the darkness,
covered in cobwebs, bruised on both knees,
there was not a single accusation or harsh word.
No "How could you be so careless?"
Only more laughter
and my ring.

THE GOOD DAY

Your alarm sounds first. I hear shower water,
doze, then feel your soft lips on my cheek,
saying good-bye just for now, as you head off
for another round of laborious union talks.

In morning's filtered light, I scoop
earth-dark grounds, add water,
fill the kitchen with aromas of two worlds,
home and a distant Guatemalan plantation.

Sipping from my cup, I gather three bowls,
serve breakfast to the other early risers,
my knees bumped by wagging tails as dogs
circle, always famished, always fed.

I peel damp sheets off the bed
after summer night's heat, float new linens
softly through the air, smooth coolness
into each crisp corner, tuck and straighten.

Picking up pen and notepad, I sit down
with yesterday's perfect metaphor. It falls flat.
Scratch it out, roll new sounds around
on my tongue, picture the polished poem.

A blue belly lizard skitters under the couch
and across my toes, its tail sacrificed to the cat.
I can save this one, scoop the wriggling body up
and release it to the relative safety of the rosemary bush.

The garden needs water. I pace between verdant rows,
touch thigh high corn, spy new potatoes poking
through rich soil, brush bugs off jalapeño plants,
watch leaves unfurl, moisture seep into the ground.

The dogs bark at the mail truck. We trot together
to the box at the end of the driveway.
I finger through bills, the surprise of a postcard
from Puerto Vallarta, friends on vacation, *hola*.

Back in the cool of my office, I escape to India,
taste chutney in the kitchen of a novel,
prepare for a Hindu wedding while parsing
each paragraph with the eyes of a poet.

The phone rings. A friend's marriage is ending.
She asks for answers, and I become a mirror
of her own wisdom, know I cannot predict
what will grow in someone else's garden.

The mercury keeps rising. I fill the wading pool
with fresh water, call the dogs, take off my shoes,
splash, dodge, play, adding the outline of my feet
to the damp paw prints scattered across the deck.

Hungry, I open the crisper and pull out fresh
broccoli, asparagus, heirloom tomatoes.
I rinse soft tofu, slice, toss it all into an iron skillet,
ready to sauté as you come in the door.

You say the union may strike. With good food
and love, I try to soothe the day's tensions,
listen to the details of conflict with management,
provide a haven from the stress of the world.

We wash the dishes by hand, move to separate corners
of the house. You unwind with a book about dragons,
I open up the past in my journal, look for healing,
remind myself I am now safe and almost whole.

At day's end, you and I savor one more cup of coffee,
watch the full moon spotlight nearby vineyards,
bittersweet sphere that shone on my father's last night
two years ago, his hand in mine, my hand in yours.

I turn back fresh sheets, snuggle in close to you.
Touch turns to passion; we merge our two histories,
create a third that is ours, both bound and free.
When I cry out in my sleep, you will be right here.

dedicated to Sabrina, with thanks to Anne Morrow Lindbergh

ACKNOWLEDGEMENTS

First and foremost, I am indebted to Ruth
Thompson of Saddle Road Press. She believed in
this book from the beginning, and proved herself to
be a wonderful editor, as well as a steadfast friend.
Thanks also to Don Mitchell for the beautiful
photograph and design of the cover.

Although writing is primarily a solitary act, I
have been blessed with a supportive community.
I am grateful for the extensive sisterhood of the
women of A Room of Her Own Foundation and
their biannual retreats in New Mexico, where I go
to refill the well. I am deeply appreciative of the
support I receive from Redwood Writers, a branch
of the California Writers Club, and the Healdsburg
Literary Guild.

A very special personal thanks to Christi Calson
– everyone needs a best friend who is also a talented
poet. An enthusiastic hug to poet Leonore Wilson,
who encourages me both with her own writing,
and by sending me email messages saying, "Submit
here!" Much gratitude to John Abbott, another
fine writer. And unending heart songs for Wendy
Dayton, who is the greatest buddy a girl could have.

I would not have survived this past year of
sometimes turbulent challenges without the
constant embrace of my writing circle, the Diamond
Flamingos: Sandra Hunter, Lisa Rizzo, Tania

Pryputniewicz, Marcia Meier, Barbara Rockwell, Ruth Thompson, Barbara Yoder, and Jayne Benjulian. I am forever buoyed by your example and by your lightheartedness.

There is a four-legged bodhisattva in my life – my service dog, Ripley – who is with me every step of the way. Although she is not much of a poetry critic, she is an essential element of any success I find on this journey.

Finally, for my wife Sabrina, without whom none of this would have been possible. You opened all doors.

About Michelle Wing

Michelle Wing has a B.A. in English from Montana State University, and an M.A. in Japanese Studies from the University of Washington. After graduate school, she received a fellowship from the Ministry of Education in Japan to study abroad, living in Osaka and Kyoto for three years.

Her poetry and creative nonfiction have appeared in *Sinister Wisdom*, *The Gay & Lesbian Review*, and several anthologies. In October 2012, two of her poems were shown in Sacramento in an exhibit at the California Museum, *Creating Freedom: Art & Poetry of Domestic Violence Survivors*, with the poem *Dreamwork* taking first place honors.

From 2002-2013, she worked as the senior staff writer for a community newspaper in the Napa Valley, the *Calistoga Tribune*. Currently, Michelle writes a monthly literary column for a small chain of newspapers in Sonoma County, California.

Raised in Montana, she spent much of her adult life in the urban settings of Seattle, Japan and San Francisco, but now lives in the country in northern California with her partner Sabrina, who never fails to ask, "What are you working on now?" She is assisted in all of her creative endeavors by her service dog, Ripley. The walls of her writing studio are painted lime green and citrus yellow, and are covered with art.

CPSIA information can be obtained at www.ICGtesting.com
Printed in the USA
LVOW13s1538020414

380016LV00004B/240/P